EXPLORING BIOLOGY

GENETICS & EVOLUTION

by
Tom Jackson

Minneapolis, Minnesota

Credits

Cover and title page, © Seregraff/Shutterstock; 3, © Anusorn Nakdee/Shutterstock; 4, © Patrick Rolands/Adobe Stock; 4–5, © theboone/iStock; 5, © Skyline Graphics/Shutterstock; 6T, © VectorMine/Shutterstock; 6B, © murat photographer/Shutterstock; 6–7, © aslysun/Shutterstock; 7T, © Public Domain/Wikimedia Commons; 8T, © TarikVision/Adobe Stock; 8B, © Public Domain/Wikimedia Commons; 9, © L.Darin/Adobe Stock; 10B, © Katakari/Shutterstock; 10–11, © Grossinger/Shutterstock; 11T, © Designua/Shutterstock; 11B, © Public Domain/Wikimedia Commons; 12M, © Emre Terim/Shutterstock; 12B, © MRC Laboratory of Molecular Biology/Wikimedia Commons; 12–13, © View Apart/Shutterstock; 13T, © ShadeDesign/Shutterstock; 13B, © Dee-sign/Shutterstock; 14, © ShadeDesign/Shutterstock; 14–15, © shironosov/iStock; 15, © Public Domain/Wikimedia Commons; 16T, © Soleil Nordic/Shutterstock; 16B, © Ali DM/Shutterstock; 16–17, © Ravil Sayfullin/Shutterstock; 17B, © Marc Lieberman/Wikimedia Commons; 18M, © VectorMine/Shutterstock; 18B, © superclic/Alamy Stock Photo; 18–19, © WHYFRAME/Shutterstock; 19T, © Public Domain/Wikimedia Commons; 20T, © Greentellect Studio/Shutterstock; 20B, © Designua/Shutterstock; 20–21, © Iokanan VFX Studios/Shutterstock; 21T, © Public Domain/Wikimedia Commons; 22M, © Ody_Stocker/Shutterstock; 22B, © Dee-sign/Shutterstock; 22–23, © Nixx Photography/Shutterstock; 23B, © Public Domain/Wikimedia Commons; 24T, © A.S.Khan/Adobe Stock; 24B, © gzorgz/Adobe Stock; 24–25, © Frazao Studio Latino/iStock; 25, © Public Domain/Wikimedia Commons; 26M, © VikiVector/Shutterstock; 26B, © Achiichiii/Shutterstock; 26–27, © koya979/Shutterstock; 27B, © GraphicsRF.com/Shutterstock; 28M, © VectorMine/Shutterstock; 28B, © VectorMine/Shutterstock; 28–29, © bbernard/Shutterstock; 29T, © German Vizulis/Shutterstock; 30, © logika600/Shutterstock; 30–31, © Sebastian Kaulitzki/Alamy Stock Photo; 31T, © Suzanne Tucker/Shutterstock; 31B, © Public Domain/Wikimedia Commons; 32M, © Daniel Beckemeier/Shutterstock; 32B, © Gorodenkoff/Shutterstock; 32–33, © MAKOTO IWAFUJI/EURELIOS/Science Photo Library; 33B, © Cmichel67/Wikimedia Commons; 34M, © Joaquin Corbalan P/Shutterstock; 34B, © Everett Collection/Shutterstock; 34–35, © Pixel_life/Shutterstock; 35T, © Chroma Collection/Alamy Stock Photo; 36M, © THE PRINT COLLECTOR/HERITAGE IMAGES/Science Photo Library; 36B, © Public Domain/Wikimedia Commons; 36–37, © Christian Edelmann/Shutterstock; 37T, © VectorMine/Shutterstock; 38T, © Anna Veselova/Shutterstock; 38B, © Andrea Izzotti/Shutterstock; 38–39, © Amy Lee/Alamy Stock Photo; 39B, © Public Domain/Wikimedia Commons; 40T, © EcoSpace/Shutterstock; 40B, © khlungcenter/Shutterstock; 40–41, © Ryan Boedi/Shutterstock; 41B, © Steve Jurvetson/Wikimedia Commons; 42, © pressmaster/Adobe Stock; 42–43, © Kar-Tr/iStock; 43, © Kittipong Jirasukhanont/Adobe Stock; 44B, © Gorodenkoff/Shutterstock; 45T, © Greentellect Studio/Shutterstock; 45B, © EcoSpace/Shutterstock; 47, © Ravil Sayfullin/Shutterstock

Bearport Publishing Company Product Development Team

Publisher: Jen Jenson; Director of Product Development: Spencer Brinker; Editorial Director: Allison Juda; Editor: Cole Nelson; Editor: Tiana Tran; Production Editor: Naomi Reich; Art Director: Kim Jones; Designer: Kayla Eggert; Designer: Steve Scheluchin; Production Specialist: Owen Hamlin

Statement on Usage of Generative Artificial Intelligence

Bearport Publishing remains committed to publishing high-quality nonfiction books. Therefore, we restrict the use of generative AI to ensure accuracy of all text and visual components pertaining to a book's subject. See BearportPublishing.com for details.

Library of Congress Cataloging-in-Publication Data is available at www.loc.gov or upon request from the publisher.

ISBN: 979-8-89577-493-9 (hardcover)
ISBN: 979-8-89577-535-6 (paperback)
ISBN: 979-8-89577-501-1 (ebook)

© 2026 Arcturus Holdings Limited.
This edition is published by arrangement with Arcturus Publishing Limited.

North American adaptations © 2026 Bearport Publishing Company. All rights reserved. No part of this publication may be reproduced in whole or in part, stored in any retrieval system, or transmitted in any form or by any means, electronic, mechanical, photocopying, recording, or otherwise, without written permission from the publisher. Bearport Publishing is a division of FlutterBee Education Group.

For more information, write to Bearport Publishing, 3500 American Blvd W, Suite 150, Bloomington, MN 55431.

Contents

Understanding Genetics and Evolution . . . 4

Studying Cells 6

Cell Structure. 8

Cell Membranes 10

DNA and Chromosomes 12

RNA 14

Reading Genes 16

Genotypes and Phenotypes 18

Cell Division 20

Meiosis. 22

Genetic Mutations. 24

Sex Cells and Fertilization. 26

Reproductive System 28

Growth and Development. 30

Genetic Engineering 32

The Theory of Evolution 34

How New Species Arise 36

Coevolution 38

Sexual Selection 40

The Future of Genetics and Evolution. . . . 42

Review and Reflect 44

Glossary. 46

Read More 47

Learn More Online. 47

Index 48

Understanding Genetics and Evolution

All living things are made of cells that are packed with unique molecules of deoxyribonucleic acid (DNA). In humans, these genes influence a person's physical features, their personality, and even their health. Over time, genes can slowly adapt to help humans keep up with their ever-changing environments. This is a process known as evolution.

Chimpanzees

Humans and chimpanzees share about 98 percent of their DNA. That is because both species descended from a common ancestor millions of years ago. As humans and chimpanzees evolved, their DNA gradually changed as well, resulting in the differences in appearance and behavior we see from both species today. One difference is that chimpanzees usually have longer jaws and pointier teeth than humans.

Chimpanzees and bonobos are considered the closest living relatives to humans.

4

Cheek dimples are thought to be a genetic trait.

The Big Five

The Big Five is a personality framework developed by psychologists to understand and measure human personality. It describes five broad dimensions of genetically inherited traits: openness to experience, conscientiousness, extraversion, agreeableness, and neuroticism. Each major trait shows how a person behaves, feels, and thinks in different situations.

According to genetic studies, about 30 to 60 percent of an individual's personality is inherited.

Studying Cells

One of the basic laws of biology is called cell theory. It says that every living thing has a body made of at least one cell—with many living things containing billions of cells—and every cell developed from an older cell. Looking more closely at cells helps scientists understand how the body works.

> Scientists who study cells are called microbiologists. They use electron microscopes to see samples in even more detail.

Light Microscopes

The main tool for studying cells is the light, or optical, microscope. It uses two sets of lenses to magnify tiny objects, allowing scientists to view them in detail. As light shines up through the sample, the first lens focuses the object into a tiny but detailed image. Then, the eyepiece and objective lenses magnify that image. This makes the picture big enough for the human eye to see.

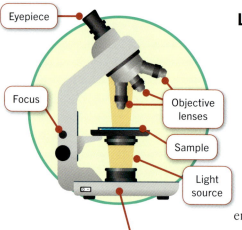

- Eyepiece
- Focus
- Objective lenses
- Sample
- Light source

A biological microscope usually has three objective lenses. Each one gives a different magnification level.

Preparing a Sample

The best way to examine cells is to place a thin slice of tissue on a clear glass slide. This slice is bathed in a droplet of water, and a see-through cover is placed on top. This holds the sample still and flat, which helps the lenses focus. Dyes are added to the water to highlight features of the sample. Salts and other chemicals can also be used to observe how the cells operate.

A thin sample allows for light to shine right through, which gives a clear picture of the silhouette of the cells.

HALL OF FAME

Margaret Pittman
1901–1995

As a child, Margaret Pittman assisted her father, who was a doctor, with his patients. Later, she attended the University of Chicago, where she became an expert in bacteria and microbiology. Pittman investigated the bacteria involved in deadly diseases, such as cholera and meningitis.

Scientists can adjust the brightness and position of the light source on a microscope to get a different view of samples.

A pipette is used to add dyes or other chemicals to samples.

DID YOU KNOW? A light microscope can see objects that are 200 times smaller than the width of a human hair.

Cell Structure

The cells of living things are made of many parts. These structures perform different functions. A gelatinous liquid called cytoplasm that can be found throughout the inside of the cell holds its organelles in place. Tiny mitochondria create the energy to power cells. And the largest organelle in any cell is its nucleus, which contains the cell's DNA and controls all its activities.

Plant and Animal Cells

Plant and animal cells have several differences. Rigid, sturdy outer layers called cell walls surround plant cells, giving them a rectangular shape. Animal cells lack cell walls. This allows them to be many different shapes and sizes. Chloroplasts, unique to plant cells, are used for photosynthesis. This is a process that turns sunlight into energy. On the other hand, animal cells get energy through cellular respiration, which is the breaking down of molecules from food.

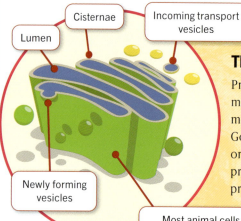

Cisternae
Lumen
Incoming transport vesicles
Newly forming vesicles

The Golgi Apparatus

Proteins are complex molecules responsible for most cellular processes. They are sorted and modified for their jobs within the cell by the Golgi apparatus, which is a folded, saclike organelle. Then, the Golgi apparatus transports proteins for usage around the cell. It also processes lipids that store a cell's energy.

Most animal cells contain only a few Golgi apparatuses, but plant cells can have hundreds.

Robert Hooke
1635–1703

In 1665, Robert Hooke used a microscope to observe a cork made from bark. Hooke noticed the cork was made up of many different tiny compartments that resembled the living quarters of monks, which were called cells. This gave cells their name and opened the door to further cell research.

HALL OF FAME

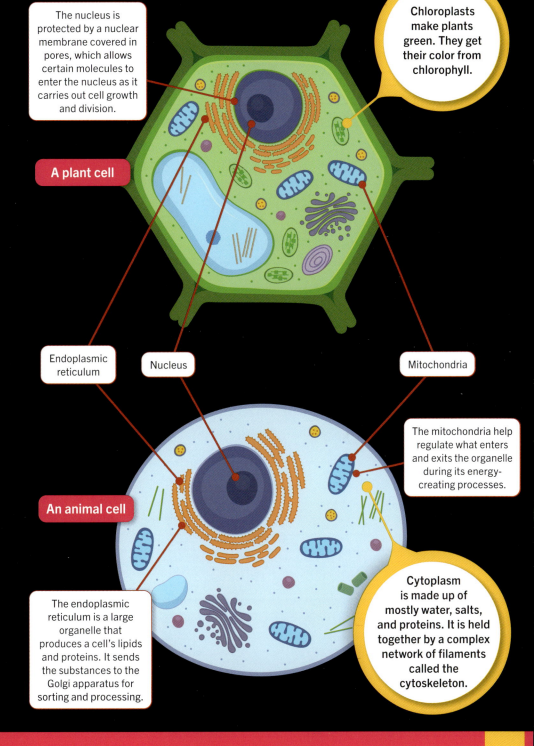

DID YOU KNOW? The average adult human's body contains around 30 trillion cells.

9

Cell Membranes

Every cell is surrounded by a thin outer layer, or membrane. The membrane is made from fatty chemicals that form a barrier against large molecules. Smaller molecules, such as water and oxygen, can easily pass through. Cells rely largely on a physical process called diffusion, in which substances naturally spread out from areas of high to low concentration. However, some cells also use more active systems to move materials around.

Cell Movement

A cell that secretes hormones or enzymes uses exocytosis (*ek*-soh-sye-TOH-sis), which is when a cell releases large quantities of a substance. The substance is discharged by the cell's Golgi apparatus. This part of the cell transports, modifies, and packages proteins and lipids into small membrane bags called vesicles. The vesicle merges with the cell membrane, and the contents are outside the cell when they are released. Endocytosis (*en*-doh-sye-TOH-sis) is the reverse of exocytosis. The material outside a cell is captured in a hollow section of the cell membrane, which then breaks off to form a vesicle inside the cell.

> Osmosis pulls water into plants. If there is not enough water in a plant's cells, the cells become soft, and the plant body wilts.

Endocytosis is used by cells that consume nutrients floating outside of the cells.

Cell plasma membrane

Secretory product

Secretory vesicle

Cytoplasm

Exocytosis

Extracellular fluid

Cell plasma membrane

Cytoplasm

Secretory vesicle

Endocytosis

10 **DID YOU KNOW?** Goblet cells secrete slimy mucus to coat the inside of the nose, lungs, and throat. In an adult human, these cells produce almost 2 quarts (1.9 L) every day!

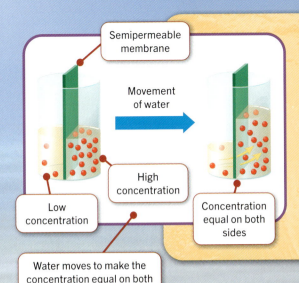

Semipermeable membrane

Movement of water

High concentration

Low concentration

Concentration equal on both sides

Water moves to make the concentration equal on both sides of the membrane.

Osmosis

Cells rely on osmosis, which is a special kind of diffusion, to move water in and out. Water can cross a cell's membrane, but other chemicals mixed into it cannot. When there is a high concentration of chemicals dissolved in the cell, water will diffuse in from outside to dilute it. If the cell is in water that is more concentrated than the cytoplasm, osmosis will push water out of the cell and dry it out.

Water is inside every cell, making it a universal solvent. All the chemicals needed for life are mixed into it.

Jean-Antoine Nollet
1700–1770

It would be impossible to understand how cells and living things work without Jean-Antoine Nollet. In 1748, he discovered osmosis by putting pure alcohol in a sealed pig's bladder that was immersed in water. Hours later, the bladder was bulging with water. Osmosis had pushed water inside to dilute the alcohol.

HALL OF FAME

DNA and Chromosomes

DNA is a chemical stored inside the nucleus of a cell on structures called chromosomes. It carries the organism's genes, which are the coded instructions on how to build new cells to grow a body.

> A human cell has 46 chromosomes, but that number varies in other species. Half of the chromosomes come from each of the parents.

Chromosomes

DNA is a delicate substance. It is protected inside the cell's nucleus, where it is kept separate from other chemicals that might damage and alter its genetic coding. The long strands are coiled up to make bundles called chromosomes. The DNA is uncoiled only when it is being copied and decoded.

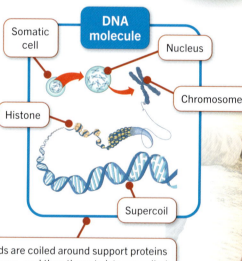

Somatic cell • DNA molecule • Nucleus • Chromosome • Histone • Supercoil

DNA strands are coiled around support proteins called histones, and then these twists are coiled many times to make a compact supercoil.

HALL OF FAME

Rosalind Franklin
1920–1958

Rosalind Franklin was a chemist who used X-rays to figure out molecule structures. DNA had been discovered in the 1860s, but 90 years later, people still did not know its shape. Franklin's X-ray photographs offered the first clue that DNA molecules are a helix—a shape like a spiral ladder. This big breakthrough allowed other scientists to figure out how DNA works.

DNA Structure

DNA is a polymer built from several units to make a helix. Ribose sugar forms the sides. There are four nucleic acids that connect in pairs to form the rungs. The order of these acids along the DNA strand spells out a four-letter code that genes are written in.

The four nucleic acids in DNA are simplified to the letters A, G, C, and T.

- Adenine
- Guanine
- Cytosine
- Thymine

Parental genes are altered and shuffled into new combinations for offspring. This is how children inherit the features of their parents.

A full set of chromosomes is called a karyotype. Each chromosome is part of a pair, with one from each parent. Humans have 23 pairs.

DID YOU KNOW? If all the DNA in your body were uncoiled, it would stretch from Earth to the sun and back 20 times!

RNA

RNA, short for ribonucleic acid, is found in all living cells. It translates the genetic information contained within DNA into the proteins that allow a cell to function. Unlike DNA, RNA is sometimes single-stranded and has shorter strands. It acts as a messenger traveling throughout a cell to regulate critical gene activity.

Viral RNA

Influenza, measles, and the common cold are all spread through viruses made of RNA. Unlike living things with DNA, the material for RNA is less complex, making it easier to mutate and replicate. This allows viruses to spread rapidly.

RNA Structure

RNA is a polymer built from a sugar molecule called ribose. It differs from DNA, whose structure is made out of deoxyribose. Like DNA, there are four nitrogenous bases that connect in pairs to form the rungs. RNA uses uracil as a fourth base, while DNA uses thymine.

RNA is constructed from a single nucleic acid strand and uses the acid U instead of T.

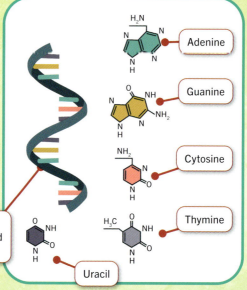

DID YOU KNOW? There are significantly more RNA molecules within the body than DNA molecules. The most common type of RNA in a cell is ribosomal RNA, or rRNA.

RNA works like a printer. But instead of translating digital information into a physical copy on paper, RNA translates genetic information into proteins.

André Boivin
1895–1949

André Boivin created the first hypothesis of how RNA impacts gene function. After discovering toxins found in bacterial cells, Boivin theorized that DNA molecules in the nucleus oversee the creation of smaller RNA molecules. These molecules influence reactions within a cell's cytoplasm. His idea led to further research that helped scientists understand RNA's purpose and relationship to DNA.

HALL OF FAME

Reading Genes

Genes are a chemical code stored in the DNA. They are made of a string of four nucleic acids: thymine, cytosine, guanine, and adenine. The order of these acids in each gene gives the recipe for making a particular protein, such as those used as enzymes or in muscles.

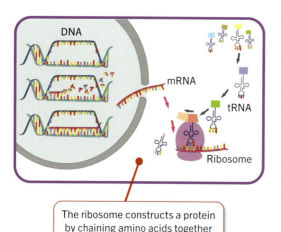

The ribosome constructs a protein by chaining amino acids together in the order set out by the gene.

Copy and Translate

The DNA code in a nucleus is copied onto a strand of messenger RNA (mRNA), which then leaves the nucleus and heads to a ribosome—the cell's protein-building factory. This factory uses transfer RNA (tRNA) molecules to translate the genetic code into a protein. Each tRNA fits with a specific three-letter sequence on the mRNA, and that sequence relates to one amino acid. The tRNAs read the gene sequences to create a chain of amino acids in the right order.

Sequence and Structure

Genetic code is a list of amino acids that show the order in which these small units must be arranged to make useful proteins. There are around 20 amino acids used in nature, and proteins can have several hundred combinations of them. This means there are vast numbers of possible proteins, but only the ones coded in genes work in the body. A DNA molecule can store these correct codes and pass them on without introducing mistakes.

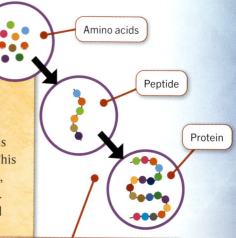

A protein is a polymer made from long chains of amino acids. A single chain of amino acids is called a peptide. Protein molecules have two or three peptides.

DID YOU KNOW? Human DNA carries a code made of 3 billion characters. This code is copied when a cell divides, which happens billions of times a day.

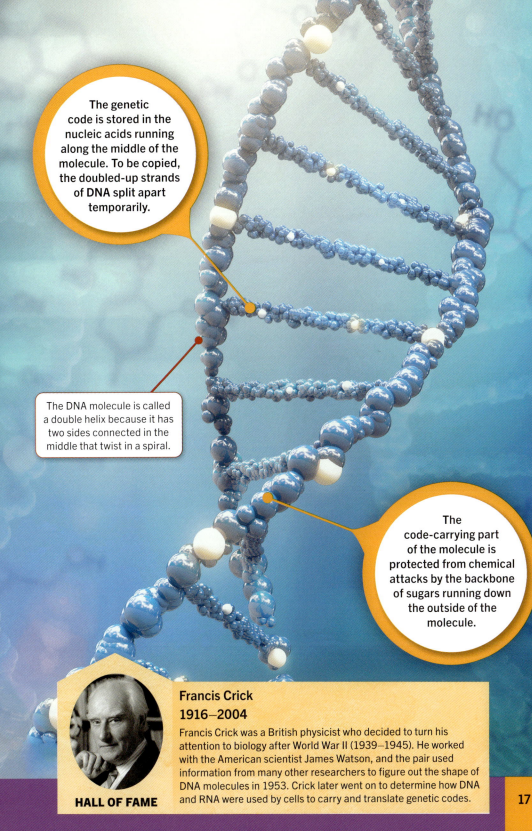

The genetic code is stored in the nucleic acids running along the middle of the molecule. To be copied, the doubled-up strands of DNA split apart temporarily.

The DNA molecule is called a double helix because it has two sides connected in the middle that twist in a spiral.

The code-carrying part of the molecule is protected from chemical attacks by the backbone of sugars running down the outside of the molecule.

Francis Crick
1916–2004

Francis Crick was a British physicist who decided to turn his attention to biology after World War II (1939–1945). He worked with the American scientist James Watson, and the pair used information from many other researchers to figure out the shape of DNA molecules in 1953. Crick later went on to determine how DNA and RNA were used by cells to carry and translate genetic codes.

HALL OF FAME

Genotypes and Phenotypes

There are two ways of understanding genes. The genotype is a record of what chemical codes a person has in their cells. The phenotype is a record of body characteristics—such as hair color—that are inherited from parents. A big part of genetic studies is figuring out how genotypes are linked to phenotypes.

Children look similar to their parents because they have inherited a set of genes from both. A grandchild and their grandparent often share the same recessive phenotype, which is something not seen in either of their parents.

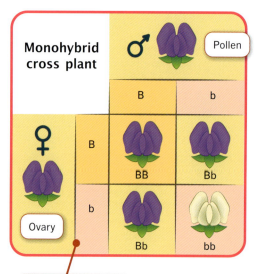

Monohybrid cross plant

Pollen

Ovary

When both parents have the dominant (B) and recessive (b) genes, three-quarters of the offspring will have the dominant phenotype. A quarter will be recessive.

Dominance

A genotype always contains two copies of the same gene—one from each parent. In many cases, the phenotype created is controlled by which version of the genes is dominant. A dominant version will always create the phenotype if it is present. A nondominant, or recessive, version of the gene is seen only if the genotype contains two copies of this version.

Codominance

For some genes, there is no one version that is dominant. If the genotype has a mix of versions, their effects are merged together to make a phenotype that is halfway between the two characteristics. This system is called codominance.

Different kinds of cat fur are controlled by a few codominant genes.

18

HALL OF FAME

Gregor Mendel
1822–1884

Gregor Mendel was a German-speaking monk who spent several years studying how different phenotypes of pea plants were passed on generation after generation. At the time, DNA had not even been discovered yet. However, his discoveries about dominance and codominance became the foundations of the science of genetics.

Black is the dominant version of the hair color gene. If people inherit this version, they will always have black hair.

A child shares half of the same genes with each of their parents. They also share a quarter of the same genes with each grandparent.

DID YOU KNOW? The human genome, which is the total collection of DNA, has around 20,000 genes. About 98 percent of the DNA in a cell carries no genetic code.

Cell Division

Cells can grow larger, but they all have a maximum size. In order for a body to grow beyond this point, its cells need to divide in two—again and again. The cell division process used for growth like this is called mitosis. It transforms one parent cell into two almost identical daughter cells. Complex cells, such as those of plants and animals, undergo mitosis. Bacteria use a similar system called binary fission.

> Between cell divisions, a cell is in interphase. During this time, the cell grows larger and organizes its chromosomes, getting ready for the next division.

Fast Growers

Cell division allows single-celled organisms to reproduce very quickly. For example, microscopic algae that float in seawater can double in number every 24 hours. Soon, there are so many that the plantlike organisms coat the water green! This explosion of life is called an algal bloom. It can spread poisons in the water and block light from reaching underwater plants.

Algal blooms are often caused by fertilizers washing into water. The chemicals make the algae grow and divide much faster than normal.

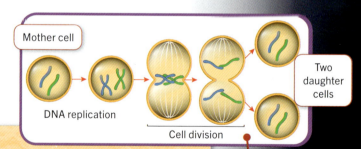

Mother cell — DNA replication — Cell division — Two daughter cells

Mitosis

Cell divison by mitosis has several phases that ensure the daughter cells always have the same genes as the parent cell. The chromosomes in the nucleus are copied into double versions with an X shape. These are lined up in the middle of the cell, and then the two halves are pulled to opposite ends. Finally, a new cell membrane forms across the middle, splitting the cell into two.

> Each set of chromosomes is pulled to one end of the cell by microfilaments anchored there, separating the two sets. The chromosomes are divided equally between the two halves.

HALL OF FAME

Matthias Jakob Schleiden
1804–1881

Matthias Jacob Schleiden was one of the scientists behind cell theory. He had started work as a lawyer, but this made him unhappy—so he switched to studying cell biology. Schleiden showed that the contents of the nucleus were always shared by the new cells. He was one of the first biologists to accept Charles Darwin's theory of evolution.

In the final stage of cell division, known as cytokinesis, a new membrane forms in the middle of the cell, dividing up the cytoplasm.

Once cell division is complete, a new nucleus forms around the chromosomes in each cell.

DID YOU KNOW? A bacterium can split in half every 20 minutes. In just seven hours, one bacterium can grow into more than two million.

Meiosis

A special kind of cell division called meiosis is needed for sexual reproduction. Meiosis makes sex cells that each contain half a set of genes. Two sex cells can merge to make a full set of genes for a new individual. This method of breeding is called sexual reproduction, and it ensures that each child has a highly varied set of genes.

Steps

Meiosis is two cell divisions in one. The first division organizes the chromosomes into their pairs before the members of each pair are separated and drawn to opposite ends of the cell. Then, the cell divides in two, creating daughter cells each with a half set of chromosomes. The next division is more like mitosis, and the two half-set cells divide again to make a total of four daughter cells.

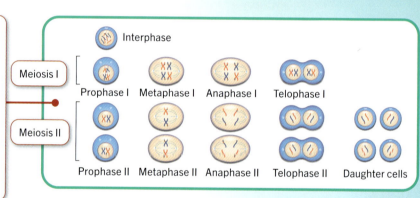

The starting cell is described as diploid because it has a full set of paired-up chromosomes inherited from two parents. The daughter cells made by meiosis are haploid, meaning they have just one of each of the pairs of chromosomes.

Crossing Over

Unlike in mitosis, in which the daughter cells always have identical genes, meiosis mixes chromosomes up to make four daughter cells with unique sets of DNA. One of the ways this is done is called recombination, or crossing over. During the first division in meiosis, the paired-up chromosomes are lined up next to each other. They are so close that they can tangle up and swap chunks of DNA.

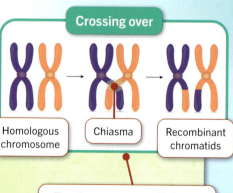

The chromosomes are X-shaped because they have been duplicated for cell division. They have two identical copies connected in the middle. During crossing over, only one of these halves swaps DNA.

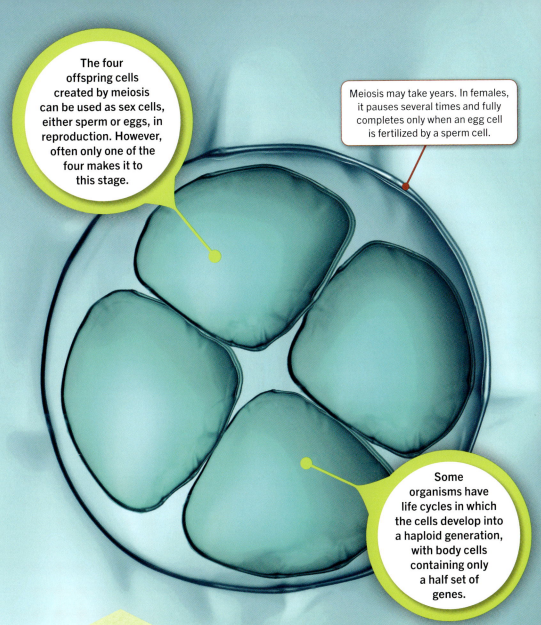

The four offspring cells created by meiosis can be used as sex cells, either sperm or eggs, in reproduction. However, often only one of the four makes it to this stage.

Meiosis may take years. In females, it pauses several times and fully completes only when an egg cell is fertilized by a sperm cell.

Some organisms have life cycles in which the cells develop into a haploid generation, with body cells containing only a half set of genes.

HALL OF FAME

Barbara McClintock
1902–1992

Starting out as a botanist studying crops grown on American farms, Barbara McClintock discovered recombination—one of the most important phenomena in genetics. While studying the chromosomes of maize, she found that they were muddled up during meiosis. Later, McClintock also made breakthroughs on how genes were read and expressed as phenotypes.

DID YOU KNOW? A female ocean sunfish, or mola mola, produces 300 million eggs each breeding season. This is the most of any vertebrate!

Genetic Mutations

Sometimes, errors occur during cell division. This causes mutations that change DNA sequences. Mutations happen constantly within the body and can permanently alter how cells function. Most mutations are quickly identified and repaired before they can cause harm, but those that are not can produce genetic conditions, diseases, and changes to physical characteristics. They also create differences within species that help them adapt and evolve.

Germline Mutations

Germline mutations occur within sperm and eggs during fertilization, leading to changes in inherited DNA. They become a part of every cell in the child's body, which can cause genetic disorders, including cystic fibrosis, sickle cell anemia, and certain types of cancer. Germline mutations can be passed down through generations of a family.

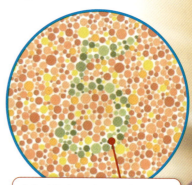

Color blindness is one of the most common germline mutations. It is often inherited from mothers on the X chromosome.

Smoking tobacco is a major cause of somatic mutations. It damages DNA and causes replication errors that can lead to the development of many types of cancer.

Somatic Mutations

Some genetic mutations are somatic mutations. These usually involve spontaneous changes to a person's DNA after conception. They affect only the cells in which the mutation happens and cannot be spread from parents to children. Sometimes, somatic mutations are caused by viruses or exposure to environmental stressors, such as sunlight, radiation, or chemicals.

DID YOU KNOW? Adult humans used to be unable to digest milk. A genetic mutation that occurred within the past 10,000 years gave most humans the ability to do so.

Down syndrome is a genetic condition caused by having three copies of chromosome 21. People without Down syndrome have two copies of this chromosome.

Scientists estimate that the average human body experiences trillions of new mutations daily. A majority of mutations do not cause significant changes or harm.

Genetic mutations happen when information is added, deleted, or substituted within the normal blueprint of DNA. This new information can cause cells to change or malfunction.

Thomas Hunt Morgan
1866–1945

American scientist Thomas Hunt Morgan bred thousands of fruit flies, intentionally altering generations through environmental changes. Eventually, a fly with a new eye color was born. It passed the physical characteristic down to certain offspring. Morgan's research helped expand the understanding of how genetic mutations are created and inherited. It also helped prove that genes are located on chromosomes.

HALL OF FAME

25

Sex Cells and Fertilization

Most multicellular organisms reproduce sexually. This involves two types of sex cells, or gametes, fusing together in a process called fertilization. The female gamete is the egg, and the male one is the sperm. Together, they make a zygote, which is the first cell of a new individual.

Human sperm is only 0.0002 inches (0.005 mm) wide. The human egg is 20 times bigger, and at 0.004 in. (0.1 mm) across, it is almost visible to the naked eye.

Gametes

Sperm and eggs are haploid, which means they have only half a set of chromosomes. Together, they produce a diploid that has a full set. The sperm has a long flagellum, which helps it swim toward an egg. It carries only an energy supply and DNA. The egg is much larger and cannot move itself, but it contains everything the new zygote will need.

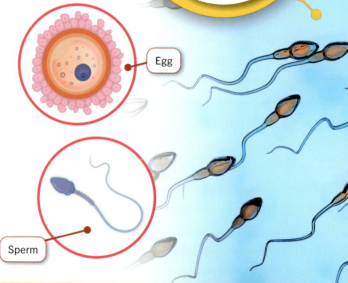

Egg

Sperm

HALL OF FAME

Oscar Hertwig
1849–1922

In 1876, German zoologist Oscar Hertwig discovered the process of fertilization by watching as the sperm and egg of sea urchins fused together under a microscope. He also discovered meiosis. During his research, Hertwig also saw that the chemicals in the nucleus were passed from cell to cell and determined this must be the way characteristics are inherited. While this is true, it took almost another 100 years to figure out how!

DID YOU KNOW? The average female human releases about 350 ripe eggs in her life. Every day, an adult male human produces about 100 million sperm.

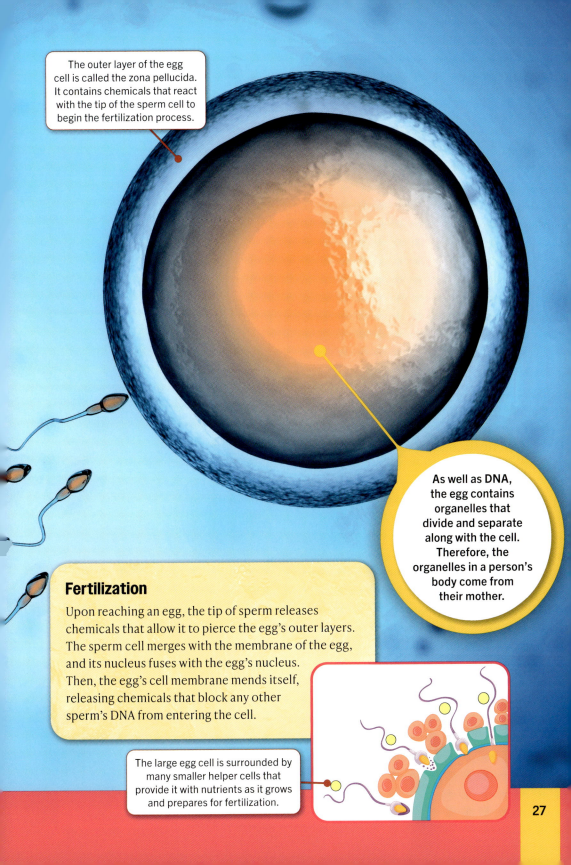

The outer layer of the egg cell is called the zona pellucida. It contains chemicals that react with the tip of the sperm cell to begin the fertilization process.

As well as **DNA**, the egg contains organelles that divide and separate along with the cell. Therefore, the organelles in a person's body come from their mother.

Fertilization

Upon reaching an egg, the tip of sperm releases chemicals that allow it to pierce the egg's outer layers. The sperm cell merges with the membrane of the egg, and its nucleus fuses with the egg's nucleus. Then, the egg's cell membrane mends itself, releasing chemicals that block any other sperm's DNA from entering the cell.

The large egg cell is surrounded by many smaller helper cells that provide it with nutrients as it grows and prepares for fertilization.

Reproductive System

A human baby develops inside its mother's uterus, or womb, before being born. This process starts when a male's sperm moves into a female's uterus and combines with an egg cell produced by the mother. Together, they make the first cell of a new human.

Doctors who look after mothers and children during pregnancy are called obstetricians. Midwives are also medical care-givers who are experts in helping people give birth.

Male Sex Organs

Sperm are produced inside the testes, which are egg-shaped organs inside the scrotum, a sac hanging beneath the penis. The sperm are transported along tubes to the prostate gland, where they are combined with liquid called semen. During intercourse, the penis is filled with blood. This makes it longer and harder so it fits into the vagina, where the semen and sperm are released.

Seminal vesicle

Prostate

Bladder

Vas deferens

Urethra

Testicle

Penis

Epididymis

The penis also contains a tube called the urethra that connects to the bladder. Urine leaves the body through the urethra.

Fallopian tubes

Fimbriae

Ovary

Uterus

Cervix

Endometrium

Vagina

Fertilization

Most multicellular organisms reproduce sexually. This involves two types of sex cells, or gametes, fusing together in a process called fertilization. The female gamete is the egg, and the male one is the sperm. Together, they make the first cell of a new individual, called a zygote.

The opening of the uterus is called the cervix. During intercourse, the cervix allows sperm in. It becomes tightly closed once a fetus starts to develop in the uterus.

HALL OF FAME

Rebecca Lee Crumpler
1831–1895

In 1864, Rebecca Lee Crumpler became the first Black American woman to become a doctor. She was a specialist in child development and the care of women and babies after birth. She worked at a time after the U.S. Civil War (1861–1865) when people who had been formerly enslaved were being freed. Many white doctors would not treat people who had been enslaved, but Crumpler provided them with care.

Ultrasound scanners send high-pitched sounds into the uterus. The harmless sounds, which are too high to hear, echo off the fetus so the parents and medical experts can see it.

Human pregnancy lasts 40 weeks, or around 9 months. At this point, the baby can breathe air and live outside the mother but still needs a lot of looking after.

DID YOU KNOW? In 2021, Halime Cissé from Mali became the only mother of nonuplets in history when she gave birth to five girls and four boys.

Growth and Development

Girls reach their full adult size around the age of 15, while boys stop growing taller at around 18. Until about the age of 24, the brain and nervous system of both will continue to develop. The fastest period of growth is while a baby is still in the uterus. A single microscopic cell can develop into a 7-pound (3-kg) baby in 280 days.

> The fetus does not breathe or eat in the uterus. Instead, it is provided with what it needs by the placenta. Oxygen and nutrients move inside the placenta from the mother's blood to the baby's.

Three Trimesters

A baby developing inside the uterus is called a fetus. Its development happens in three-month stages, or trimesters. In the first trimester, the fetus develops all its body parts and organs. The fetus's body is mostly fully functional by the end of the second trimester. If it is born around this time, the baby could live—as long as it gets good medical care. The third trimester is devoted to growth and adding fat under the skin.

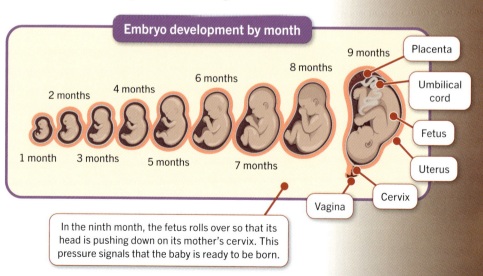

Embryo development by month

In the ninth month, the fetus rolls over so that its head is pushing down on its mother's cervix. This pressure signals that the baby is ready to be born.

DID YOU KNOW? Only 5 percent of babies are born on the exact day they are predicted to be due. The rest arrive early or late.

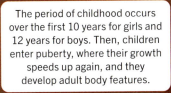

Childhood

In the first year after birth, a child will double in height and triple in weight! By the age of two, they are half their adult height. But a child may not reach half their adult weight until they are about 10.

The period of childhood occurs over the first 10 years for girls and 12 years for boys. Then, children enter puberty, where their growth speeds up again, and they develop adult body features.

For the second half of pregnancy, the fetus has a covering of fine hairs and slime. This falls off just before birth.

The umbilical cord connects the fetus to the placenta. This is cut after birth, and it falls away, leaving only a belly button.

HALL OF FAME

Cleopatra the Physician
1st century CE

Aside from being a doctor and writer, not a lot is known about Cleopatra of ancient Greece. She wrote one of the first books on gynecology, which is the medical study of the female reproductive organs. Cleopatra also wrote extensively on other ailments suffered by women and suggested using medicines, such as roasted horse teeth, mouse droppings, and deer bone, as cures.

Genetic Engineering

Scientists have figured out ways of changing the characteristics of various life-forms by editing their genetic codes. Most often, they engineer simple organisms, such as bacteria and yeasts, but more complex plants and animals are also being altered. Genetic engineering can be used to make better medicines and cure diseases.

> This mouse has been given some genes from a jellyfish that allow the creature to glow in the dark. The mouse's skin now makes the glowing chemicals.

Medical Breakthroughs

Genetic engineering can be used to make medicines and other useful chemicals on a large scale very cheaply. Insulin, a chemical used to treat diabetes, has been genetically engineered. It is not possible to make pure insulin from raw ingredients in a factory. However, genetic engineers have added the gene for insulin production to a bacterium. The bacterium is grown inside a vat, and it produces the complex chemical in large amounts.

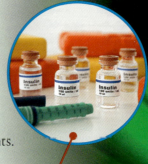

> Some people who are diabetic cannot make their own insulin to control their energy supplies. However, the insulin made by genetic engineering works just as well.

> Plants can be engineered to withstand being sprayed with herbicides that are used to kill weeds or other unwanted plants growing nearby.

GMOs

Genetically modified organisms, or GMOs, are plants and animals that have been created by genetic engineers. GMOs are made for several reasons, but the most important is producing food. Genetically modified crops can grow well in places where regular crops could not. However, some scientists worry that these plants will breed with wild plants and create dangerous pests and weeds.

32

The genes added by genetic engineers can be passed on to the next generation just like natural genes. GMOs must be carefully controlled so that their added genes do not escape into the wild.

These glowing chemicals could be used to target cancers and other problems in the body so that they can be spotted very early.

Jennifer Doudna
Born 1964

There are several techniques for editing DNA sequences, but the one used most often today is called CRISPR, which is short for clustered regularly interspaced short palindromic repeats. This system was developed by Jennifer Doudna, along with her collaborator Emmanuelle Charpentier. In 2020, the pair received the Nobel Prize for their work. CRISPR takes a system used by bacterial cells to add DNA to any sequence of genes.

HALL OF FAME

DID YOU KNOW? Genetically modified goats have been given the genes for spider's silk. The milk from these goats contains large quantities of silk.

The Theory of Evolution

The organisms that live on Earth today were not always here. They evolved from earlier life-forms, many of which have now become extinct. Evolution is a system of change that is driven by a process called natural selection.

Fossils

We know that different animals and plants lived long ago because of fossils, which are the remains of living things that have turned to stone. Fossils provide a record of how life has evolved slowly over many millions of years. They also help show how the environment has changed. These changes are the major force that drives evolution. Simple life first appeared at least 3.5 billion years ago. All life that exists today evolved from those early life-forms.

> This frog has failed to avoid being captured by a predator. Its genes and characteristics will not be passed on to the next generation.

> The plesiosaur was a reptile and relative of the dinosaurs. It lived in the oceans around 100 million years ago. It evolved from an older animal that lived on land.

HALL OF FAME

Charles Darwin
1809–1882

English naturalist Charles Darwin is famous for his book *On the Origin of Species*, published in 1859, in which he set out his theory of evolution by natural selection. At the time, many people were shocked by Darwin's ideas, but many years of research proved his theory that life is able to change gradually to adapt to new habitats and conditions.

Natural Selection

All living things compete with one another for food and living space to survive. This struggle drives evolution by using a process called natural selection. No group of organisms is identical; there is always variation. Some variations are better fit for survival, and these individuals do well and have many fit offspring. Organisms that are less suited for their habitat die without reproducing. This means that useful characteristics gradually spread through a population—and so species evolve slowly over time.

Charles Darwin thought up his theory of evolution by natural selection as he traveled the world on HMS *Beagle*. On his voyage, he saw many unusual animals and plants.

This heron has inherited genes that make it a successful hunter. The better it is at hunting, the more likely it will be to pass on those fit genes to the next generation.

Webbed feet are a useful characteristic for animals that swim. Frogs that live on land have evolved toes without webs.

DID YOU KNOW? Charles Darwin probably got many of his ideas about life-forms from his grandfather Erasmus Darwin, who also wrote about evolution.

How New Species Arise

A species is a group of organisms that look similar and live in the same way—and, most importantly, can breed with one another to produce the next generation. Every living species today evolved from an older one that is now extinct. All closely related species evolved from the same common ancestor.

African savannas have a lot of room for large animals and many opportunities for different species to live in their own way.

Adaptive Radiation

New species develop from common ancestors because natural selection allows different groups to adapt to changing conditions. This leads to adaptive radiation, in which related species take on different characteristics to survive in different ways. Darwin's finches living in the Galapagos Islands provide a good example. They all evolved from the same ancestor but now have different beak shapes, so they can eat varied foods on the islands.

Birds with chunky beaks eat hard seeds, while pointed beaks are used for snatching insects.

HALL OF FAME

Georges Cuvier
1769–1832

Experts in fossils are called paleontologists. They work to find the long-gone common ancestors of today's species. Georges Cuvier was a leading figure in the early days of fossil science. In the 1790s, he showed that fossils were old species that had gone extinct, rather than ancient versions of modern animals. This discovery changed the way scientists thought about life on Earth.

DID YOU KNOW? More than 99 percent of all species that have evolved on Earth have now become extinct.

Zebras share a common ancestor with horses and donkeys. Together, this group of horselike species are called the equids.

Speciation

There is more than one way that a new species can diverge from an older one. The most common is called allopatry, in which a species becomes divided in two by geography. Natural selection means that they evolve in different ways, and by the time they mix again, these groups have become two species. Sympatry is when a new species forms within the older one as some members specialize in targeting a new source of food and diverge from the rest.

Sympatry

Allopatry

In these two examples, one species becomes two. Natural selection can also transform a whole species into a new form of life.

There are dozens of different antelope species living in this part of Africa. Each one is adapted to eating a particular kind of food in a particular habitat.

37

Coevolution

Natural selection changes organisms so that they fit better with the environment around them. This leads to some amazing effects. In coevolution, the survival of two species is so closely linked that they evolve together in some way. In convergent evolution, completely different organisms end up adapting in the same way to their habitats.

Mimicry and Camouflage

Animals evolve disguises that work in their habitat. Camouflage allows a creature to blend in with the colors, tones, and patterns of its surroundings, so it cannot be spotted by predators or prey. Mimicry is when an animal evolves to look like another animal. Mimics often pretend to be a more dangerous species to scare off attackers. Groups of poisonous species may evolve to look alike so they all benefit from the same warning signals they give to predators.

This gecko is camouflaging against bark. Outside of this habitat, its woodland disguise would be useless.

Convergent Evolution

There are multiple examples of how natural selection has come up with the same answers for surviving in a habitat. Dolphins and sharks are distant relatives. Sharks are fish that evolved 450 million years ago, and dolphins evolved from land mammals around 50 million years ago. However, both have the same general streamlined body shape.

These two species have evolved similar body shapes. However, the dolphin's tail flukes are horizontal while the shark's tail fins are vertical.

This flower has evolved to attract butterflies. It has a wide and flat landing area for the insects to stand on while they feed on nectar and collect pollen.

The monarch butterfly is bright orange as a warning to predators that its body is filled with a poison. Several other butterfly species use the same hue to send the same message.

Insects and plants have coevolved. Many flowering plants rely on insects to transfer pollen from one bloom to the next.

HALL OF FAME

Mary Anning
1799–1847

Mary Anning grew up on the southern coast of England near a region of cliffs that are full of fossils. She became a fossil hunter as a child and made some very important discoveries. In 1811, she found the skeleton of an ichthyosaur. Ichthyosaurs were marine reptiles, and through convergent evolution they looked a lot like sharks and dolphins. Anning's fossil finds inspired other scientists to study extinct animals, leading to the discovery of dinosaurs.

DID YOU KNOW? The world's largest flower, the stinking corpse lily, has evolved to smell of rotting meat instead of a sweet perfume.

Sexual Selection

Natural selection is a process that allows only the organisms best suited to their environment to survive. How does this explain why some animals have features like bright feathers or huge tails that make it harder for them to survive? The answer is a special kind of evolution called sexual selection.

> A male bird of paradise needs to spend a lot of time and energy getting noticed among the dense leaves.

Sexual Dimorphism

There are often obvious differences between the males and females of certain species. Features particular to one sex may be used to signal fitness to members of the other. These features may include anatomical curiosities that have no obvious use for survival, such as colorful tails or huge antlers.

> This male duck is out to impress the female duck, showing off his plumage. She will choose which male bird to mate with.

> Females that mate with big-headed males like this will produce male offspring that also have wide heads. In this way, the sexually selected feature spreads through the population.

Big Heads

This stalk-eyed fly has a very wide head with bulging eyes on each side. The males use this feature to figure out which one is in charge and has the right to mate with a female. They line up head to head, and the male with the widest stalks wins. This system prevents risky fights. The loser will leave and look for another mate. Next time, he might be the winner in the same head-to-head competition!

This bird relies on a courtship display to attract a mate. The females watch the males show off, choosing the best performing mate.

These spiraled tail feathers catch the eye, but they also make it harder for the bird to fly. Only the fittest birds can stay strong and healthy despite these unhelpful features.

HALL OF FAME

Richard Dawkins
Born 1941

Richard Dawkins, a British professor of zoology, is most famous for introducing the public to the ideas of neo-Darwinism, sometimes called the selfish gene. These ideas emerged in the 1960s and seek to explain how everything that happens in evolution is driven by the need for DNA to make copies of itself. Natural selection works at the genetic level, and living things are just survival machines built by DNA to help it copy itself.

DID YOU KNOW? Deer stags use antlers to signal who is the fittest. The Irish elk is an extinct deer species that had antlers almost 12 feet (4 m) wide.

The Future of Genetics and Evolution

People continue to evolve as time passes. Many scientists predict that future humans will grow taller and have longer life spans due to advancements in nutrition and health care. Some think that thanks to modern transportation, the global population will look more alike as different groups of people from around the world come into contact more frequently.

Advanced Health Care

Scientists are working toward improvements in DNA technology that will allow them to better correct genetic mutations before they cause harm. They also hope to create personalized medical treatments based on individual genetic makeup. These advancements could lead to better disease management. They may even allow us to save people from diseases once thought to be incurable.

In some parts of the world, the average human height has increased by around 4 in. (10 cm) since the beginning of the 20th century.

Cancer

Cancer is one of the leading causes of death in the United States. Early screenings, improved treatment options, and decreases in tobacco use have contributed to a 33 percent drop in the cancer death rate over the past few decades.

In the United States, cancer is the second-most common cause of death. The first is heart disease.

Review and Reflect

Now that you've read about genetics and evolution, let's review what you've learned. Use the following questions to reflect on your newfound knowledge and integrate it with what you already knew.

Check for Understanding

1. What is the Big Five? Why did psychologists develop it? *(See pp. 4-5)*

2. What does cell theory tell us? *(See pp. 6-7)*

3. Name and describe three structures in the cells of living things. *(See pp. 8-9)*

4. What is osmosis? *(See pp. 10-11)*

5. Name three facts about DNA. *(See pp. 12-13)*

6. In what ways is RNA different from DNA? *(See pp. 14-15)*

7. How is genetic code related to proteins? *(See pp. 16-17)*

8. Describe the difference between a genotype and a phenotype. *(See pp. 18-19)*

9. What are the two main types of cell division? Which kinds of cells use each type? *(See pp. 20-21)*

10. What causes genetic mutations? What are two kinds of genetic mutations? *(See pp. 24-25)*

11. Name the two kinds of gametes. What does it mean to be haploid and diploid? *(See pp. 26-27)*

12. Name three parts of the male reproductive system and three parts of the female reproductive system. *(See pp. 28-29)*

13. What happens during each of the trimesters of pregnancy? *(See pp. 30-31)*

14. Describe one way people have used genetic engineering. *(See pp. 32-33)*

15. Explain the process of natural selection *(See pp. 34-35)*

44

Making Connections

1. How are mitosis and meiosis alike and how are they different?

2. In what ways is genetics relevant to the study of natural selection?

3. Choose two people mentioned in the Hall of Fame sidebars. What do they or their work have in common? How are they different?

4. How does the study of cells relate to genetics and reproduction?

5. Compare and contrast the processes of cell division with the process of natural selection.

In Your Own Words

1. One hundred years ago, scientists knew much less about cells, genetics, and evolution. How might human life have been different without the knowledge we have now?

2. The book describes some examples of sexual selection. What other examples can you think of?

3. Humans will continue to evolve through natural selection. Which human traits do you think will persist and which might become less common?

4. In your opinion, which person described in the Hall of Fame sidebars did the most interesting or useful work? Why do you think so?

5. If you could join a scientist studying genetics and evolution, which areas would you choose to study? Why?

Glossary

amino acid an essential nutrient containing several chemical elements

bacteria a large group of single-celled microorganisms, some of which cause diseases

cell the basic unit of plants, animals, fungi, and microorganisms; each cell has a nucleus and is surrounded by a thin membrane

DNA short for deoxyribonucleic acid, the chemical ingredient that forms genes; parents pass on copied parts of their DNA to their children, so that some of their traits are also passed on

enzymes chemicals that speed up or slow down the ways in which substances react with each other

fat a chemical substance that the body produces to store energy

genes combinations of chemicals that carry information about how an organism will appear and behave

habitats places in nature where plants and animals live

membrane a thin, flexible layer of tissue around organs or cells

molecules small units of a substance made up of two or more atoms

nucleus the central part of a eukaryotic cell, which controls its function and stores its DNA

nutrients substances that provide food needed for life and growth

organs groups of tissues that work together to do a specific job

organelles parts of a cell that do a job

organism a living thing, such as a plant, animal, fungus, or single-celled life-form

predator an animal that feeds on other animals

proteins molecules that are needed to strengthen and replace tissue in the body

species a group of similar-looking organisms that can reproduce together

sperm a male reproductive cell that combines with a female's egg to produce a new baby

tissue a collection of cells that look the same and have a similar job to do in a body

vertebrate an animal with a backbone

zoology the study of animals and animal life

Read More

Banks, Rosie. *Inside Evolution (Inside Modern Genetics).* New York: Rosen Publishing, 2022.

Braun, Eric. *Working with DNA and Genetics (Technology Triumphs).* Huntington Beach, CA: Teacher Created Materials, 2025.

Holt, Amy. *DNA under the Microscope (The Inside Guide: The Microscopic World).* Buffalo, NY: Cavendish Square Publishing, 2024.

Learn More Online

1. Go to **FactSurfer.com** or scan the QR code below.
2. Enter "**Genetics Evolution**" into the search box.
3. Click on the cover of this book to see a list of websites.

Index

amino acids 16

bacteria 7, 15, 20–21, 32–33

cell division 16, 20–22, 24

cell membranes 10–11, 20–21, 27

cells 4, 6, 8–12, 14–28, 30, 33

chromosomes 12–13, 20–26

codominance 18–19

coevolution 38–39

convergent evolution 38–39

cytoplasm 8–11, 15, 21

deoxyribonucleic acid (DNA) 4, 8, 12–17, 19–20, 22, 24–27, 33, 41–42

diploid 22, 26

disease 7, 24, 32, 42–43

dominance 18–19

egg 23–24, 26–28

endocytosis 10

enzymes 10, 16

evolution 4, 21, 34–35, 38–42

exocytosis 10

fertilization 23–24, 26–28

fossils 34, 36, 39

genes 4, 12–16, 18–20, 22–23, 25, 32–35, 41

genetic codes 16–17, 19, 32

genetic engineering 32–33

genetics 4–5, 12, 14–19, 23–25, 32–33, 41–42

genotypes 18

Golgi apparatus 8–10

habitats 34–35, 37–38

haploid 22–23, 26

meiosis 22–23, 26

microbiologists 6

microscopes 6–8, 26

mitosis 20, 22

multicellular organisms 26, 28

natural selection 34–38, 40–41

nucleus 8–9, 12, 15–16, 20–21, 26–27

organelles 8–9, 27

osmosis 10–11

oxygen 10, 30

phenotypes 18–19, 23

polymers 13–14, 16

pregnancy 28–29, 31

proteins 8–10, 12, 14–16

ribonucleic acid (RNA) 14–17

sex cells (gametes) 22–23, 26, 28

sexual reproduction 22, 26, 28

sexual selection 40

species 4, 12, 24, 34–41

sperm 23–24, 26–28

transport 8, 10, 28, 42

zygote 26, 28